PAVLOV'S CAT
Poems and other Stories
TD Euwaite

PAVLOV'S CAT
Poems and other Stories
TD Euwaite
Copyright © 2008 Tangled Web Press

Edited by:
Elaine S. Polin
Dr. Christine Sukic
Sheryl Brotbeck

Foreword by:
Elaine S. Polin

Cover Design by:
TD Euwaite

Photo of M&M by:
Elaine S. Polin

PAVLOV'S CAT
Poems and other Stories
Copyright © 2008 Tangled Web Press

ISBN 978-0-6152-3710-7

Tangled Web Press
PO Box 233
Shawnee Mission, KS 66201

http://blog.poetsofmars.com

PAVLOV'S CAT
Poems and other Stories
TD Euwaite

FOREWORD

TD Euwaite is a true Renaissance Man. The poet, who feels he was born at least a century too late, deserves to be numbered among the Masters. "When is my time, past or forthcoming? Where is my place? Here or There?" These questions and the title of his book hint at his versatility and the depth of his knowledge of poetry, past and present.

He has posted some 1,000 poems on the Internet in the past year alone. They are preceded by intriguing questions, leading his readers into a realm of mystery, humor and wonder. His proverbs and questions have stimulated thought, argument and creativity among Internet poets from all over the planet: "Poems should be nurtured, not neutered." And "If I dream a dream— and it does come true—Who's to blame?"

His poetic messages and forms include humorous "thingies" about everyday life as well as dialogue and shape poems, new legends and free and tightly structured verse. A vast body of work tickles, delights and amazes TD's audience.

The poems often convey messages in the guise of irony: "Cornplanter knows that peace is fleeting. He understands that we have fear because many things are frightening. Cornplanter tells the stories so we can learn to face our fears." So does the poet.

In addition to legends and new words, TD has created several new poetic forms. The Converb, a proverb with a twist, has become a favorite of his Internet followers. The Trigee, a three-in-one poem, is probably his own favorite. Readers have imitated these creations dozens of times.

His poems may sometimes be humorous or ironic, but he is serious about his work and teaches others to be serious as well, demonstrated here in a favorite Internet post from 2008:

> Monosyllabic elements juxtaposed
> Rudimentary linguistics investigated
> Intellectual processes scrutinized
> Phonic dynamics dissected

His first book, OH WHAT A TANGLED WEB, POETRY OF THE INTERNET, published in 2008, is already being taught in some university classrooms as an example of modern poetry. It is a compilation of poems written by real, virtual people.

In PAVLOV'S CAT, POEMS AND OTHER STORIES, the reader is treated to poems by the creator of a movement connecting the virtual and real worlds through the power of his pen and his keyboard.

Like all great artists, the poet suffers occasional angst, but expresses it in his own oblique fashion: "Damp, the pond for frogs...Damp, by God..." Or, in a Trigee:

> I spun around.............the lamppost
> crashing headlong......was upside down
> in the mirror...............this must mean
> I was inverted.............the world was right.

However, the reader never suffers, but accepts TD Euwaite's poetic gifts with laughter, awe and deep appreciation.

Elaine S. Polin

INTRODUCTION

I build a poem by stacking ideas one onto the next. Once in a while, I actually plan the ending. For the rest, I allow the characters and scenes themselves to take me to the finish. I simply meander down the streets and pathways of imagination and describe the things I see and hear.

As the old saying goes, "I have been from Maine to Spain to Austin to Boston..." My father was a pilot and a golfer. He always made sure that his next set of orders were to somewhere with civilized golf. During his 45 years in the air, our family lived in Japan, England, the US and Guam.

My mother is a poet and English scholar. She is the one who introduced literature to me and the rest of the kids. We grew up with Homer and Shakespeare. We read the classics and went to Sunday school religiously. We spoke and wrote proper English because we were being drilled constantly by an authority.

The Internet is the place where my poetry finally began to flower. After I stumbled onto the Yahoo! Answers forum by accident, I started posting poetry there in May of 2007. I had no idea what was about to happen, falling into a virtual well of talented people exchanging poetry and critiques. I found beginners reaching out and experts holding their hands.

After being slapped around by a couple of English teachers, I hit the books. Picking up where Mom had left off 30 years earlier, I dived headlong into Eliot and Cummings. I reread all the Kipling and Poe that I have loved as a young boy.

I read and wrote and listened and taught. A year later, I have over 700 new compositions in my resume. My friends Christine and Elaine are the ones who convinced me to put some in a book. You may blame them if you don't like it.

TD Euwaite

THE CHAPTERS

Chapter I

THE CONDITIONED CAT

GOD'S GIFTS*

God gave hands
To the fisherman
To cast nets
O'er blue water
To bring forth
The bounty
That His hands
Left within

God gave eyes
To the wanderer
To tell beauty
From darkness
To seek out
The garden
Only His eyes
Comprehend

God gave us
To each other
So we'd
Stand together
Knowing
The future
By His will
Unfolds

* The first poem I ever wrote.

I FELL INTO THE FIRE

I fell into the fire,
...burning embers charred my soul
Hands reached out to hold me down,
...so cold, so very cold

The heat, the ice, the timed turmoil
...how can they both be one and the same
And my pity and shame
...shown to the world as it turns

THE KANSAN

Midnight's come and gone,
and so the sailor's red sky warning,
brings the dawn
with West Wind mourning
cross the prairie
grasses burning,

April does not let you sleep,
as shutters bark and shingles leak,
the rain comes down in sheets and sheets,
and all's asleep, save one who watches
South by Southwest,
South by Southwest...

WAFFLE HOUSE

I go to the Waffle House
each morning at five,
I like to watch her get out of her car,
I can see the apron under her coat,
I can feel her fire,

In that hour before the rush,
amidst the crackling of bacon
she fixes her hairnet just so,
I don't care if she gets it everywhere
because some of it, some of her,
will be in me,

The waitresses like to act pretty,
Tips make or break a day on the floor,
Not for Molly, no no,
She's the waffle machine Queen,
Batter me with love.

PORCHLIGHT

Where is the finest
Free designer
Artist's daughter, loving father
The one who draws me as I truly am

She's coming home from broken promise
With her talents and the chorus
Singing songs that she
No longer wants to hear

Come cry your lonely sorrows
Cupid's arrow and tomorrow
With a token you can
Ride the tears away

Do not forget the home that wept
As you slept inside, she kept
Laughed at the silly fears
Counting years
And then tonight
Has cried

STRETCH THE CANVAS TIGHT

Stretch the canvas tight
Add layer after layer of white
Then Brown-Black the base
Paint a foundationless home
Detached from Earth and floating
Paint a legless man waiting
Paint a fruitless tree arching
And a light just off the center
With chair and guitar akimbo
A Daliesque windchime
Of dream pieces scattered and displaced

A.P.O.

Wrap the brown paper
Two times, and staple
Tape up the corners
With clear cellophane

Address the white label
Afghani high desert
To soldiers off guarding
A peace never known

Send them a garland
And mountains of chocolate
A note that you love them
The flag that you wave

Remind them to watch
Out for each other
And come home tomorrow
This time, to stay

WATER

Falling down around the edges
Pooled droplet domes
A crease in the sand
Trickling, flowing
Directionless meandering
Joins the enjoined, tributary
To stream, and river's torrent
Engulfed, saline fusion
Sea to Ocean current
Challenger Deep
Evaporation

DANCING WHITE GOWN

Spin around
Dancing white gown
Petticoat promenade
Wind me up and around

White ribbonned hair
Brushed cheeks in the breeze
Perfumed skin
Air slowly breathed in

Whirl me around
Dancing white gown
A touch of her hand
Softly, gently captures me

A chill up her arm
Enraptures me
While turning around
The dancing white gown

ORANGE TABBY

The cat makes no valueless sounds,
As he looks for the hounds,
The crows, the mouse,

Puts no foot down without thought,
Upstairs, downstairs, glaring stares,
Nine-lived feline, stalking hunter,

Tree limbs, porch swings, couch cushions,
Fearless jumper, fierce tiger claws,
Purring, pouncing, parading pufftail...

THE ACCOUNTANT'S SOUL

The bottom of the line is where I work,
Where the dollars meet the donuts, I hope,
My poetic verse, the General Ledger,
Fiduciary trusts, for your pleasure,

I hear the mournful cry of Aging Lists,
Places where defaulted credit lives,
I leave behind a heart that wants to bleed,
And balance what I want with what I need.

CARRY ME DOWN

Carry me down to the river Jordan
Wash my face in the current so strong
Marry my faith with the healer Jesus
Take my body and sing this song
Hallelujah!
Oh good Lord—Hallelu, ooh jah!

Fold my hands across my chest
Wrap me in a clean white linen
Hold me up to the Lord like Lazarus
Let him save me from this death
Hallelujah!
Oh good Lord—Hallelu, ooh jah!

Bring along my bag of silver
Give it to the priests proclaiming
Wings of angels do not take me
Let me stay until tomorrow
Hallelujah!
Oh good Lord—Hallelu, ooh jah!

TOM HALL

Tom Hall was a gentleman
Outspoken orator
Suave sophist
Aristocrat heir
Bowed to the ladies
Hat tipped to a passerby
Buttoned up shirt
White boutonnière

Mary Ann Holloway
Home for the holiday
Prim and proper
Quiet, reserved
Cast an eye toward him
Captured a vision
All too careful
To look unconcerned

Tom remarked
How the weather was
So very hot today
Tugged at his collar
Loosened his tie
Mary Ann fanned
And sipped at lemonade
Inside their hearts
Clandestine plans made

PAVLOV'S CAT

In the early years at
University of Saint Petersburg
Professor Pavlov developed an idea...

"We turn on zee light and zee
cat will salivate in anticipation
of zee reward...now, hit zee switch!"

"What is wrong, Mister Pusspuss,
don't you want zee nice piece of liver?"

WHERE ARE THE CHILDREN

Where are the children
Where's my garden
Please, I beg your pardon
Turn your hooded face to me
And explain the reasons why

Where is my wife
My true lover
Where's my son
And our two daughters
Do not point your shriveled hand
And beckon me

I've got to finish my first novel
And the driveway needs fresh gravel
I do not have the time to go with you

Go back to your dominion
And your honorary minion
You cannot take me with you
My work is far from through

I've prayed for Heaven's absolution
Not this horrid retribution
What can I do to earn another day

CHECKMATE SERIES NO. 1
THE BLACK PAWN

Identical, these eight on line
Turned on a lathe
This fodder,
A thin defense against the White
With one move, one direction,

The labyrinth they build
Before Knight and King
For the Queen,
Making gaps for Bishops and Rooks to
maneuver,

Attacked or impasse
Diagonal thrust
Soon the board is clear of you,
You wait in a pile for
End Game.

CHECKMATE SERIES NO. 2
THE WHITE QUEEN

She must move first
Thin vanguard of Pawns
Or Knights leaping forward,
She's crowded in tight with faith and family
And two turrets flanking,

She waits, unable to take a step herself,
then pushes a Pawn, by two,

The Black Bishop
His Knight alongside riding
They wait without pity
But first, Black must front her Pawn with Pawn,

She answers, pulling faith's White Bishop
into the slot to chastise,

Cross or Black Crown
The Black King ponders...
Pawns will not quench his insatiable thirst,
As Power Pieces can,

He sees her there, and her actionless King
She builds a nice wall of players,
But, he will have her,

The pitched battle's gridlocked on off-colored squares,
Nowhere for succor or solace
No part or portion off limits,

White moves, Black moves
White attacks, Black defends,

Who will win, in the end, the first move offends...

CHECKMATE SERIES NO. 3
THE BLACK KNIGHT

Upon my steed I wait for White to come
I must, as Black, in order, last, you see,
A chess game is a formula of sums
Impatience only fogs the mind in freeze,

And now the time has come for me to move,
When ordered to preserve the King and Queen,
As Pawns around White Castles disapprove,
Or strike at ghosts in places where I've been,

Hopscotching cross the battlefield of squares
I move in ways no other pieces can,
Of me, your faith and fort become aware,
There is no way to know where I will land.

CHECKMATE SERIES NO. 4
THE WHITE ROOK

Tall Tower
Waiting for the Queen to show the way

She's the power
I'm the sturdy, sturdy, sturdy rock spire

Stand for hours
Until she's ready to make moves toward the black line

I devour
Knights' and Bishops' black power

CHECKMATE SERIES NO. 5
THE BLACK BISHOP

See a black square on the board
One piece is all it will hold
Opposed by white sides times four
At corners, colors are told

The two Black Bishops align
Each has a color they sing
Her Bishop's angles designed
White to the right of the King

And as the game starts to turn
Diagonal strikes take a toll
Defenders easily learn
Advantage comes and goes

CHECKMATE SERIES NO. 6
THE WHITE PAWN

Identical, these eight on line
Shining miniatures of Bishop and King
Striking at will
...since granted first move

"Aggression or Death," the White Credo
You're handed the advantage, now take it
No mistake, Black King wants you dead

Move forward, move fast, move en masse
The game will not last long after
You are piled aside the board...

CHECKMATE SERIES NO. 7
THE BLACK KING

I've aligned to your regulations
My Queen, and Bishops stand waiting
A thin wall of Pawns
Easily moved, sacrificed

I play last, defensive
My Knights and Rooks guard
Against the coming White hoard
As you advance

Each step is made to counter
Whatever piece you're after
I know your only goal
Is taking me down, down

I stand as you deliver
Blows from hands that quiver
At the thought of letting me
Take the game

CHECKMATE SERIES NO. 8
THE WHITE KNIGHT

Charger, guarder
Piece leaper,
Pawn sent to
Deep sleeper,

Queen keeper
Measure meter
Risk taker,
Defeater.

CHECKMATE SERIES NO. 9
THE BLACK ROOK

Black rock granite,
Hammer Man,
Damn it!
Steady, slow,
Thunder rolls,
In place
Between power throes.

CHECKMATE SERIES NO. 10
THE WHITE BISHOPS

Guarded motives, make them wait
Abide, abate, behind Pawns' gate
As furies build, strain and complaint
All for the King, they hesitate,

One is two, and two are one
Before the battle has begun
They write a writ can't be undone
Of what to take, and when to run,

They strike and glide in angled thrusts
Free from carnal needs and lusts
These two pieces forge a trust
And do the things they know they must.

CHECKMATE SERIES NO. 11
THE BLACK QUEEN

A polish meticulously kept
A position most jealously guarded
She waits for no Knights and Kings
She plans beyond faith and family

A movement quick and agile
A sharp steely slice in diagonal
She turns left and right, turns the knife
She fights a man's fight, yet is frail

A cleanly defined silhouette
A clearly designed attack strategy
She plays to subvert and overthrow
She's the power and will to control...

CHECKMATE SERIES NO. 12
THE WHITE KING

How has it come to pass
That he is here on my second line
How has the match
Gotten so out of hand

If he is here as I am
Eye to eye in End Game
Why does he wait
Why does he taunt me

He likes to march
He likes to mark off the squares
He likes me cornered and toothless
Laid bare

Checkmate!

Chapter II

THE MANX TALE

MR. TIPTON

Mr. Tipton, expert horticulturist,
B.S. in Botany from Bancroft,
Girls wiggle giggling past his tulips,
Aloof, untouched by their perfume,
Sets about his planting routinely,

Petticoat rose petals, sunlit maidens,
Unruffled, he scribes in his journal,
Hair ribbons dangling lilac in color,
Briars and thorns next to bare white flesh,
He wonders if they will be careful,

Claire and Amanda in the high phlox,
Pungent beehive nectar saturated air,
Undaunted, he gathers his fork and spade,
Songbird ballad, sunset amber behind silhouettes,
Scientific mind, unflappable, hopes they return tomorrow.

UNDER THE CANOPY

I am here,
In the forest,
Waiting by,
A trickling fall,

Where I stand,
It seems forever,
Here I am,
Dogwood, small,

Flowering,
Pink and ivory,
Underneath,
An emerald veil,

I wait for you,
In the shadows,
Branches spread,
Along the trail,

Here I stay,
A pathway marker,
For the ones,
Who hear the call,

I wait here,
By the river,
At the flowing,
Waterfall.

WHAT THE SPARROW KNOWS

The sparrow knows
The snow is coming,
Squirrels running, careful, cunning
Stashing walnuts in the garden
Storm clouds finish summer's pardon
Fall in colorless display,
Fades away to shades of gray,
In winter's way.

PRAIRIE CEMETERY

Sunflowers follow the warmth of you, glowing,
Summertime vibrant alive colors flowing,
Sandy soft grass mounds, stalks and stems bowing,

Picnic place perched under shady persimmon,
Plates all arranged, and manors forgiven,
Peace, perhaps passion, appetite driven,

Laughter for lunch under crystalline sky,
Lazy lament of our chances passed by,
Long ago lovers, under prairie grass lie...

THE LONG AND LONESOME JOURNEY

I'm on a long
And lonesome journey
Far away, yet far to go
I can't remember
How long I've traveled
I can't turn round
I can't go home

The time has come
For me to ponder
Where I've been
Where I will go
Am I to lead
Am I to follow
Together all
Or all alone

THE TOWER

The tower walls are green with mold
No candle light is seen
A parapet that no one walks
My foggy, shrouded dream

I wait along the banks of Spey
I call the name, Colleen
For thirty years, I've haunted here
In hopes my soul to clean

BLACKSTONE MANOR

Hounds whelp at the walls
Of old Blackstone Manor
On the moor, through the fog
A candlelit window
Lady's soft whisper
A call to her love

Come back to me, Darling
From Majuba Hill
In the land of Transvaal
In South Africa
I wait for you here
While the fire's still burning

Many years later
I still see you, lover
Officer's sabre and buttons of gold
I know you fought bravely
My young handsome lover
I know that another
Will soon come to call

SMALL CRAFT

Dash the bow deeper
Into the blue water now
Now hold it steadfast
On a course to the wind

Lash down the netting
And batten the hatches
Make ready for rolls
Rig all for high seas

Splashing green foam in
The Pilot House flooded
Away, ye young lads
The Sea beckons all

Over the side boys
Into blue water
Pray that St Andrew
Will hold out his hand

THESE ARE THE WORDS FROM THE BOOK

These are the words from the book,
Regard them, guard them,
Carefully mark them,

Recite the words from the book,
Respect them, reflect them,
Project them on high,

Remember the words from the book,
Passed down, passed around,
Passed in stone,

Spread the words from the book,
In translation, in notation,
In exalted explanation,

Content with the words from the book,
With no demand to understand,
The writer's hand.

I WILL NOT TURN...PINK

On a midnight walk,
Down a moonlit pier,
appears,
a creature from the sea,

He says, "Hey man can
you give me a light?"
What a peculiar sight...
indeed,

I says, "Fish, I quit,
Smoking sea weed,
But still,
You're standing here
with me,"

Fish to fish, out in the air,
It would be safer in the water,

So, I step inside, to hide,
From the big pink fish,
At the end of the pier,
With a cigar and beer,

Lobster red, lemon yellow,
Clarified butter, austere,
"Can he be...
poached?"

SELECTIVE SAINTS

Mary and all the Martyrs
A bravery we no longer notice
Christ-like compassion's passé
For the sake of profit
All God's laws are quite vague

A golden pathway requires investment
Who will manage it?
Men of money and power charge by the hour

Hooray for the Red, White and Blue
All for you...and yours...but what about theirs?
Sculpted hair, tattoos and a chrome plated booger

Look at me!
Mary and all the Martyrs?
Is that a band?

WICKED, WICKED BOY

Shadowless forms know no sunlight
no reflection, no silhouette
When asked for a song, they sing nocturnes
lamplight's splintered duet

Hurried along by the master
crimson sunrise, morning rain
Quickening steps hold the darkness
to my door stoop, comes the pain

Into the box, Doppelganger
hide from the daylight, and rays
I'll leave you there until midnight
then on our flight, through the haze

SIXTH GRADE THIRD DEGREE

Mr. Hoppernokker will see you now...

"Come in, Son. Sit down."
He spoke and spoke but none of his
seeds could take hold on the rocky crag of my wits.
All I saw was the oar.

Not for propelling canoes, paddling kayaks
This device is ferule in nature
I'd felt its sting before
There it hung, like an old friend
...waiting.

Why do they do this, a soft comfy couch...
like a condemned man's last meal.
...and then, the words...

"This is going to hurt me
a lot more than it will hurt you."

MY NEW GIG

I had a dream where I was part
Of the Pop Machine
Not the bits where money goes
Or polished nice and clean

I am where the work is done
With cans of every kind
I simply do dispense the things
So brightly advertised

INTRO TO ANCIENT LIT

Ms. Henchly waved her stick
while shouting in an accent thick,
Homer and the Iliad
until our feeble eardrums bled,
Relentless without pity, pander,
Virgil, Horace, and then Menander.

TIMES, THEY AREN'T A CHANGIN'

One thousand years ago
Ethelred unready paid
Thirty thousand pounds to the Danes
For two years of peace from their raids
Perhaps if he'd not defica' ted
In the Baptismal Font, and his bed
Olaf Trygvasson's fleet would have fled
Instead, Ethelred
Ordered them all massa'cred
And on St Brice's they celebra' ted
Foot games with heads of the Viking dead
Sweyn Haraldsson so enraged
Engaged in campaign to win Engal'end
Thrown back in the sea again and again
By Edmund the Ironsi'ed

LOST GODDESSES

I heard a voice
Amongst the noises
Clear message
In the forum
As the Senators
Rambled on and on

A claim of notice
Full and focused
Our fallacies
...in motion
Memorandum to
A goddess
Hear what he has spoken...

"We've lost Minerva
Shamed Diana
And poisoned Cybele's water
What kind of father
Has Caesar become?"

DR. OLDMAN

The sorry old sap still mumbles
the classics as if any of his students
were listening...he has no idea
what their dreams are of...

Free from interruption, his placid
meandering through Homer is a
solitary sojourn...except when his
thick accent makes a funny...

He rides in the horse, again,
in a battle with Agamemnon. The
rage and wrath of Achilles...
fall on incurious ears...

DEAR HOMER

Dear Homer,

We have evaluated your manuscript. We
believe there is commercial viability in your
story and have decided to publish it in our
upcoming periodical, En Globus Cyclio, with
the following changes:

1. Instead of trade relations causing the war, we
want a mad-naked woman to be kidnapped and
stolen across the Aegean, only to fall in love with her
captor.

2. During the war, we want Ulysses to build a giant
hollow horse, fill it with Kung Fu guys, then sneak it
into the city under the guise of a gift.

We hope these adjustments meet with your approval.

Sincerely,
Trojan Press

THE COST OF DOING BUSINESS

Anthony hurries down the hall
with the new supply order.

"4,000 lions!" he screams
as he bursts into the office
of Cracus Grabus, the head
of wild animal procurement.

"They've lost their friggen'
gourds up there!" the chief bellows.

"I told them league expansion
would kill the games. Why in
hell do they need a coliseum
in Judea?"

"What are we going to do, Sir?"
Anthony asks.

"Have you called
Beasts-R-Us in Nubia?"

"They are shipping 900 today."

COMPACTED MAYFLOWERS

In the name of God, Amen,
In men, with names unwritten
For our sovereign, James,
Virginia we claim, for the King!
In the year...Anno Domini 1620,

Covenant and combined together,
Civil Body Politick named,
Proclaimed, order and preservation,
We hereby enact, constitute and frame
A just set of laws of equality,

At Cape Cod on November 11th
A promise we make to the King,
Your obedient and submissive colony always
All for thee, Lord of Brittan, France and Ireland,
Our Sovereign, fret not, we're so far away...

LITTLE BOY CHILD

Play with life,
My little boy child,
The road goes on,
For miles and miles,
Stop to chase snowflakes,
Leapfrog, catch rain,
Kiss the miller's daughter,
Search for treasure in the cane,

The more times you reach
Into pockets of time,
For a token, or ticket,
A piece of red twine,
Or pause to throw seed
From the hen keepers gate,
The less time you'll have
To fear, loathe and hate,

These moments spent well,
My little boy child,
Turn days into lifetimes,
Inches to miles,
Strength comes from vision,
Wisdom from smiles,
Let fools seek out fortune,
March rank and file,

For when you do reach
The toll master's gate,
No icon of gold
Scepter, or crown,
Will pay for the passage,
Like this love you have found.

EUWAITE HERE, MISTER!

I was a terrible slacker
Mrs. Smith, and her stick called "Brat Whacker"
Me in the hall, the kids had a ball
Hearing the crack of her smacker!

Chapter III

THE NATURE OF THE BEAST

LITTLE GREEN VINE

Hi, I'm, a little green vine,
I want to find, a fence to climb,
I want to grow, twelve feet long,
Careful not to touch the lawn,

Spring, seeds, the start of me,
I think I'll go, climb that tree,
On my tips, buds will grow,
I'll put on a flower show,

Here she comes, water can,
Sunshine Lady's, garden plan,
She likes me, her little green vine,
I dance in the wind in summertime,

Hi, I'm, a little green vine,
Twisting, running trailing kind,
Black Eyed Susan and Sweet Pea,
They cannot keep up with me,

Watermelon's big and slow,
Pumpkin vine has time to go,
And the Morning Glory's blue,
Can't grow as fast as you-know-who,

So, I'm, off to climb,
A trestle or a bench this time,
She likes me, her little green vine,
I'm here and there and all entwined.

Hi, I'm, a little green vine,
I look for spots of bright sunshine,
Up the wall or through a hole,
I can even climb a pole,

Yellow flowers opening,
Favorite of the Bumble Bee,
Hummingbirds like nectar sweet,
I am everybody's treat,

I will grow until the Fall,
Auburn speckle covered wall,
And the most important thing,
Spreading seeds to grow next Spring.

MIDNIGHT

Two silly gooses
Honking their love songs
Keep me awake
With their trumpeting air

Moon out my window
With Petrograd magpie
Light as a feather
With lunatic flair

Out of my window
Sprinkling bread crumbs
So they will sing
Serenades uncompared

All of my lifetime
The muses delighted
Bringing me riddles
And notes for my prayers

Now, I must leave them
So others may follow
To the end of the journey
They have prepared

COLD WINTER

Follow the tracks of the rabbit
Snow makes him an easy prey
For dinner, we'll have hasenpfeffer
If my aim is good.

The children used to cry for Peter
And beg me not to shoot
Now that times are nicht goot,
Better than eating a boot.

SMALL POND

Nightcrawler,
worm wiggler,
Bluegill tantalizing
dangler.

Cricket chirper,
Sunken bug,
Carp catcher
critter.

Bobber knockin'
big mouth,
B'ass buster,
Brain fish—too smart for TD.

TEMPTATION

Why is there an earthworm
down here in the water?
What is this string and hook attached?
Do they think I'm stupid?
Still, that fat juicy worm looks pretty GOOD!!!

FORTY SEVEN ANTS

Forty seven ants caught a caterpillar nappin'
Tried to lift him up this big old mountain
Gathered all around
Didn't make a sound
Pick'd him up, lift him up, carried him around!

Up to the top of the anthill's where they want him
Hold him, grab him, ain't no slumping
Up the mountain fast
Near the peak at last
Driven little ants, one's lost his pants!

Almost to the top, close to the summit
Two let go and away he plummets
Down the hill they go
Their dinner getting cold
Now he's at the top... "Gonna' need a bigger hole!"

YOU BUG ME

I'm the bug, little bitty body
Down in the rug with the dander and dust
Hiding from vacuums,
And famished arachnids
All the fuzzy critters that can eat me up

You won't notice me, almost microscopic
Singing to you, but your ear's so far away
Watch out for me, in your high heel pumps
"What was that sound?"
"What was that crunch?

I AM FROG, HEAR ME RIBBIT

I am Frog, hear me ribbit
By the babbling brook I sit
Girls come by and kiss me all day long
Hoping I will turn into something

But I'm just a frog
No silly lap dog, paper fetcher
Slipper chewer, not me

I wanna be a free
Tree frog, not a bump on a log
Or salamander
Fly flippin' tongue wagger

I wear green with pride
Inside amphibian
Prince to be, in a dream
Time and Toad croak for no Frog

WAVES

Waves make waves
Beaches are wave killers
Blue and green are wave colors
Black and Tan is good as sand
There's lappers and splashers
Serving seagull buffet
Smells like sea spirit
Sounds like Nirvana

CAT AND MOUSE GAMES

I fooled that cat again
Got me a lump of cheese the size of a thimble!
He snored, so bored with chasing me
You know, twice I tried
And thrice, I hide
But, this time, the cheddar treasure is mine!

I'll curl up behind the fireplace
Watch the snow as it's falling
I'll remember all the mouses
Lost in the house of this cat
Big fat orange sunnamagun!
You've had your fun,
And me?
Tonight, I'm eating.

THE BATTLE OF BOSTON IVY

The ivy grows along the wall
The rock will break and chips will fall
While splitting bricks and mortar run
The creeping vine will have its fun

With whacks I wave my machete
Turn leaves and twigs to confetti
We battle this way, day after day
Still, nothing will come from the terrible fray

The rain and wind sing a chorus
The Roses and Holly ignore us
In Spring, we dig until wet and all muddied
Autumn we finish, hands worn and bloodied

AMERI-KU

Pear tree perched swallows,
Feast on flying flutterers,
Cabbage and watercress,
Will not mourn the loss,
Of such insatiable appetites.

FROM SPRING TO FALL

And the sun warms the path
As the willow buds
Squirrels in the trees, finding love
Time of the mud and the crocuses
Soft ground between toes...squisheses

A walk on what sometimes is firmament
Slips down the granite rock steps
Landing on something less permanent
Flesh and bone, piercing tones
Ouch! Can you rub me with liniment?

AND YOU CLIMB

As you climb and rise through thinning air
Your breaths become short staccato gulps
The pains of burning muscles ache
Each step you make takes you higher
Still you climb

The crest is up above the clouds
Past eagle's nest and edelweiss
A place unseen by those below
Beyond the scope of common eyes
Still you climb

The shrine of this legend is golden
Not from ingots lifted to the summit
On the backs of ordinary men
The shine of this temple
Is you climbing
And you climb

SURVEY

The Tulips sprouting
Thin robins probe soft ground for breakfast
The imprints of my steps fill with moisture
As I survey the garden, and plan a season

The Hollyhock
And Foxglove already reaching skyward
I shift the rocks so she will move her black snake nest
And the bees, will they come back this Spring

The army ants
And beetles battle for the flower mound
Where Nasturtium crawls along the ground
And I plan another Summer showcase

PATIENCE

Where is he?
That big orange fatty
What ravaged Ethel so mercilessly a fortnight ago

Fat Leon, thinks he's a lion, this one
Many a mouse's fate's been sealed
With his morning meal

That dustbroom tail swishing
And him wishing for a mouthful of
Mouse fooled

I smell him
Canned fishes and his wishes done
For fun, he hunts us little ones

Here I wait, not cat bait am I
I not get et
I be
The smart mouse

THE CHASE SCENE IN GREEN

No myth, this dragon, spotted green on green
Monitor of Guam's think tangan-tangan,
Low and sleek, undulating nose to tail,
Silent, cunning hunter of shrews,
Only the boar, and man, his equal,
Bursts onto the trail with speed alarming,
Northwest Field, unhunted for decades,
A dangerless oasis where life can mature,
Five feet long, this one!
Two hundred pounds, thirty miles per hour,
I yielded the path, letting him lead,
Weaving the palm tree slalom I could not follow,
I slowed to a stop as the canopy lowered,
He moved through the jungle as the master,
I stayed to watch him slip out of sight,
Yet he turned to me, as if to ask,
 for another motorcycle chase.

WA ZA ZAT?

I caulked up that window
The one Alfred Hitchcock installed in our bedroom
That howls at the slightest breezes
And when the spring storms come
It's like there's a Foley stage under the bed
But I'm not really su'scared
I have Leon and Felix and Sheryl
When things get really upturned
We have tea and muffins

DRY GULCH

There is a short and narrow passage
Along walls orange, clay strata
Deep cut, twisting canyon
Empties onto a dry wash
Useless gravel panned through for gold two hundred years
Only as a pathway now, without a stopping place
For delusions of fortune

IN THE TALL GRASS

The bull moose bawls and barks
Grunting and scratching
There's a cow in the air

The brown bear hears a likely lunch
The hunter wants a trophy
The bull moose is red eyed and straining

The cow, grazing in the tall grass
She chews away at blade and root
As the hungry cravers design

—shot, mauled, gored or mounted
Which will be her life, which will be her death

BUSY BUZZ BUZZ

If
I was
A bug
I would buzz for you
I'd fly around, and walk upon your food

If
I was
An ant
I would crawl toward you
And tell my friends, where you've spilt the sugar

If
I was
A wooly worm
I would eat your herbs
Except at your place, the herbs fight back

LINES OF DEMARCATION

Black Mud Dauber glides in the breezeless air
In and out through a hole in the screen I never patched
Between the windows, he builds his adobe hacienda
And now there are two, busy do-it-yourselfers

The long brown hollow slowly turns gray
As the mud dries and solidifies their lair
I respect the claim they have made
I regard the stinger they brandish

Next Spring, I will clean away the abandoned nest
For now, live and let live in a peaceful coexistence

OVER-FED GOPHERS AND RACCOONS

I dig and I dig
Sweep pebble and twig
Past turf and topsoil
To the brown yellow clay
Where the limestone goes
From here to Montana
And I dig

I move rocks
With hammer and blocks
And I stack, flat on flat, where
Beetles and black snakes
In the cold crack resting places
Cool air lingers
And I move

I plant seeds
For rodents and me
And argue over tuber and bulb
Rabbit's bad habits
Bushels of berries and beans
For all the fat furries
And me

OUCH!

Book says mining bees
Normally do not sting you
I need a new book

THEY LOOKED REAL TO ME

There is a moment
When the stolen
Ornamental flowers
Pass from free to fallen
Photograph them then
Remembering when
They meant something

BREAKFAST SAFARI

The rutted road rolls underneath
My old Ford truck as it rumbles
We stumble down forgotten paths
In search of some more fresh Morchella

Mushrooms unlike little Alice's
No daydream in my morning endeavor
All I want is some scrambled eggs
With sautéed shallots and scallions

DAISY

circular patterns
droplets cast
wake and wave, pond ripples
skipping stone
cool afternoon
asleep in a dream, elastic

CON-VERB

A Con-verb (the opposite of Proverb) is meant to be a rude little squawk about anything that bothers the author. There are no rhyme and meter requirements. The only rules in Con-verbs are: they must be short and to the point, they must have a barbed tale or other sharp stick at the end.

CON-VERB #1
LONG LEAF

Cigarettes
became the bad guy
when John Wayne
got lung cancer.

*****

CON-VERB #2
ORANGE JUICE

How much money
Do you need to spend
To get away with murder?

*****

CON-VERB #3
GREED KILLS

How can a company
Report a loss and
Pay a dividend?

TOY BOAT TOY BOAT TOY BOAT

off with clothes
into the blue tub water
here we go, into the wash
bubbling up, foaming with squeaky cleanness
rubber boat, and soap on a rope

we scour and scrub
splash and rub
toweled and tidy
powdered body
ready for...you decide...

MOTH MATH

"Bernie! Get over here!"

Bernie flutters away from the lovely blue cashmere.

What's wrong, Boss?

"Have you seen these numbers?"

It's been a slow month. Don't worry, mildew is down, so the new suits will not be going to the cleaners anytime soon.

"You think the new stuff is silk blend?"

Sure, the economy is not that bad.

MOUSEY DICK

"Smell the tuna in the air, lads?"
"Thar she blows," whispers Ahab.
(Ahab is a very wise old mouse)
"The big orange fatty..."
(Leon is our orange tabby cat)
"Look lively Mouse Mates."
"It's cat we fish for today."
(He has tied a string to the vacuum cleaner switch
and baited the other end with catnip attached by Velcro)
"Steady...steady..."
YAWW HISSSSS PTHTTT YAWW!
"We've got the hairy beast!
Stand By For Suction!"
vvvvvvvVVVVROOOMMMMMMMMM!

GEOM

There are many names for these "Shape Poems." I call mine the
GEOM. Many of them are simple squares, triangles and sawtooth
waveforms. In these two, I have tried to draw a picture that goes
along with the subject.

GEOM I

I
seen
the grey white shape
steely **EY**ed fish swishes by
in the surf, he trolls for his breakfast
surfer dudes on a platter, with red gravy
seal a meal, yum........................**I, I, I,**
I watch them
salmon and otter.....................**I, I, I,**
for his delight as he bites bites bites
the smart fish school you
dry am
I

GEOM II

                    ! >>>>
I have a friend on an ...Island >>>>>>
A weekend with her.....!....
Breakwater Jetty.........!......
Slipping out of.............!.......
The Channel................!.........
Waterborne.................!...........
You glide....................!.............
Sailing.........................!...............
Along............................!...................
Mastering waves, she and I on her sloop
Sail
Move,
Commanding all that we see as we sail......

STILL LIFE

Why do you lay
stretched out
on sun-baked
sand?
You look tired.
How long has
your flesh
been missing?

MAY AND THE SUNLESS SKY

Hear,
the thunder clapping
Eastward roll
from the hills
down onto
the greening
valley floor.

Rain,
it pours out
on the wheat and corn,
wheat and corn

Black,
the sky and lighted
with lightning rise,
hypnotize

12/21/2012

Nostradamus tells us of
The ending of the world
When time comes to a grinding halt
Humanity unfurled

Mother Shipton tells us all
The carriage has no wheels
Battles fought by flying men
And ships that swim like eels

Mayans understood the date
A thousand years ago
Spinning round their calendar
Are simple truths unknown

In all the books of ancient times
The Bible to I Ching
The oracles alarm the world
And we don't hear a thing

01/01/2013

"What was that?"
I think it was hell and damnation.
"Where's the sun?"
I think it comes up in the north now.
"When?"

ONCE BITTEN

I bend low, so slowly,
careful to move, not the air,
I watch her, focused, deliberate,
Her breakfast of my blood,
She drinks of me and I bleed,
I swat the mosquito,
and lose no more,
And I wonder
if
she
has left inside me,
the White Nile.

THE CHICKEN OF BABYLON

Caught and penned
and now
I'm poultry.
No more sultry
co'ck carousing.
With contented hens
arousing.
Downey soft
egg layers
lounging.
Strut and crow
else cracked
and stewing.
Now,
I must now do
what
Rooster's doing.

THE DIFFICULT QUESTIONS

"What are Alates?"
That's what you are, son.
"What does it mean?"
It means you will have sex with the
Queen then die a few minutes later—
"Worker Ant doesn't sound so
bad after all."

HOW SAD FOR THEM

Tawa saw the children
by an ordinary fate forlorn.
He plucked the colors
from many things
and put them in the bag.
Tawa then shook the bag
and butterflies appeared.
They sang beautiful songs,
but the birds complained
to Tawa. He understood the
songbirds' plight
and took song away
from the butterflies. That is
why they remain silent.

Hopi Legend

STORY TIME

The thunderous herd of butterflies
rolls down from the hyacinth. We tremble not
as the air shakes none.

The terrible tormented snails charge
as Kipling's Light Brigade
is told in the gazebo by Aunt Charlotte.

Lemonade quaffs a parched niece and nephew
as the caterpillars spin a silken hammock
for their afternoon nap.

Gilgamesh and Josaphat
are new names for two old cats
that sleep in the shade nearby.

Fairies that look just like dandelion seeds
float in the afternoon air as the tales
of foreign travails flow down from Olympus.

And Auntie's flask gives her a splash
as she reads to us of sprites and spirits on ice.

THE VERSHITZER KENNEL CLUB POETRY COMPETITION

"They're bringing in the Iambic Group now. What a gorgeous pack of animals we have on display tonight, Bob."

"That's right, Nonbob, this is the crème de la menthe, the top of the hump, the dog of the dogs."

"Let's hear from our first animal, the Bichon Frisé."

bark BARK bark BARK bark BARK bark BARK bark BARK.

"What tones, what candor, a canine Shakespeare.
What do you think, Bob?"

"You hit my nail on the head that time, Nonbob."

"Next, we have the Irish Wolfhound."

bark BARK bark BARK bark BARK bark BARK bark BARK.

"The classic Celtic brogue; the sorrow, the pity...
and, our last animal, the Orange Tabby."

meOW meOW meOW meOW meOW.

"This certainly ushers in a new day here at Vershitzer, wouldn't you say, Bob?"

"I tell you, Nonbob, this is the most disgraceful display I've ever been witness to—if you don't count that time my wife..."

"That's it from Murgdeson Square Garden.
Goodnight, Doggie World!"

FINITO

What has the cat gotten into this time
Things do not look right
He's got that smirk on his face
He thinks I'm dumb
But I see through his not-so-clever
charade
And the little grey tail between his teeth
flails like Ahab's beckoning arm

Chapter IV

THE CAT INSIDE SCHRODINGER'S BOX

MY SHOEBOX

What wondrous things my old shoebox holds,
Spilling all over with poems and prose,
Napoleon's there, and Genghis the Khan,
Shillelagh, Hockey Stick, Sorcerer's Wand,

I'm riffling through it, you see,
I've lost something in there, of me,
I can't seem to find it,
I know I designed it,
It's probably old—and fil'thy,

Close to the bottom, it's there,
Next to a lock of my true love's hair,
The edges are worn, with creases, and torn,
A sad look, forlorn,
There in Mom's mirror,
Is me.

A PARADE OF TOYS

Rubber dragon
Painted with fiery red eyes
Fierce looking on the shelf
Out of reach, so I just watch

G.I. Joe, camouflaged warrior
Action figure with batteries not included
You can make him fight
With the ten dollars
You got for your birthday

Plastic B-2 Bomber
A child's wish for global domination
Can quietly deliver death horrific
But you must make the sounds yourself
Wait and see what Santa brings

AK-47
A gift for my son
Hopefully he won't kill anyone

DREAM MACHINE

Humm...buzz...ding ding ding
Oh what a beautiful thing, ring ring
Look out world, here comes me
Riding along
On my dream machine

With a monotonous ring, ding, ding
Spitting oil,
Gas and steam
What a colorful scene, ding ding

Skies of brown, seas of pink
Oh what a beautiful thing, ding ding

Fish are floating in the sea
Don't blame me
Ding ding ding ding

CRITIQUE

That's...not...art!
It does not make my head hurt
It doesn't make me do the ding dong dance

That's...not...poetry
It failed to make me jump the ledge
There is no fun inside of this for me
No guns, no knives nor bigotry

That's...not...painting
There's no fire, there's no evil, there's no hating
You call this work of yours a triumph
This silly bit of hope and guidance

WARRIOR'S LAMENT

I hear tomtom calling
Dark forest echoes
I feel drums beating through tall grass

On crest a signal fire
Warns of great danger
Ride away to spirits pointing

I see a totem gesture
Sign pathways ending
I hear Grandfathers
From herds up in the sky

CURTAIN CALL

Act 1, Scene 1.
Curtain up, queue the chorus.
Hope the audience adores us
Playwright's words,
Command performance.
Dramatic, comedic, somber, uproarious.

Act 2, Scene 2.
Long flowing hair.
Time's turning leaf.
Canine clown adds comic relief.
Laughter, tears,
Intermission,
Whispered critiques, disbelief.

Act 3, Finale.
Heroes lost in a storm.
Nerves tingle, hearts warm.
Dying embrace, a kiss.
Applause, curtain calls.
Not a dry eye in the room.
Success!

A YAQUI WAY OF KNOWLEDGE

Stop at the sign, stop,
At the sign,
Reverberations, broken concentrations,
Non-vehicular representations,
In silencing the internal voices,
Long marches, narrow corridors,
Repetition of noises.

Eighteenth attempt,
We are now stopped,
Visually past,
The sign in my mind,
No echoes. No shadows. No images. No sound.
I have stepped into nothing,
With a quick flip into the ceiling,
I am flying,
The buttress supporting a new reality,
The new observant component.

I see me, and then he and me,
But he's an it,
He actually is like,
Sea Urchins,
Pulsating spikes,
Central core, spherical gaseous layers,
Penetrations,
Separations,
Amalgamations,
A working model of the Universe,
Contemplation, experimentation, extrapolation,

An instant of seven minutes.
How will I ever explain?

GO AWAY!

Away with sidewalk children's chalk pictures
Their dragons, red wagons, and undersea creatures
I haven't the time for word games like Scrabble
I must carry on without Psychobabble

The taxing of mental and fiscal audacity
Burdening process and wallet's capacity
I must not slow down to dibble and dabble
I must carry on without Psychobabble

THE CONUNDRUM

Colors on my palette run together,
The canvas waits for me to draw a line,
With problems in pigment I can't measure,

Layering the base, it seems forever,
The white on white on white with no design,
Colors on my palette run together,

Paint a bird, but do not start with feathers,
The flight is something harder to define,
With problems in pigment I can't measure,

I need a masterpiece I can treasure,
A benefactor's impatient deadline,
Colors on my palette run together,

As if the easel and I were tethered,
I do not have the courage to resign,
With problems in pigment I can't measure,

As shadows fall, I cannot tell whether,
The images I see are even mine,
Colors on my palette run together,
With problems in pigment I can't measure.

TINKERER

"Pots and Pans! Pots and Pans!"
The tinker's out front with his cart...
"Tea kettles mended! Fireplace swept!"
Whatever needs done, he can,

"Clean up the yard, stitch a hem!"
He's a crafty old geezer, is he,
"Solder or paste! Old knobs replaced!"
Bring your things broken to him,

"Garden weeded! Fix a screen!"
No riddle gets the better of him,
"Doors unlocked! Steps replaced!"
He's got a good eye, a good bean.

I GOT A DD ON THE RORSCHACH TEST

Moth,
No, Mom?
Maybe Mohair Sweater?
Dragons?
No, they're not real
Must be an escalator, Sigmund
An Urn?
No, vase, or is it vauze?
It's not a frog?
I know that.

IS NOTHING SACRED*

Open your books.
Let's begin...
Here at the Church of the N,
Nothing is said,
from beginning to end
...and long lists of Nothing are read,
Again.

At the alter we,
Friends of the N
Old gray men,
Reaching in,
Praying for Nothing,
pray again
...Nothing is sacred,
Amen.

Sing along.
Sing the long, slow songs.
Hear the words,
of Nothing, hear N
Here,
in the end,
remembering N
...Rejoicing in Nothing,
Join N.

*A tribute to Gahan Wilson

CAFÉ MACABRE

Neon OPEN sign tilts in the window,
Torn green umbrella, flower pots empty,
Café Macabre lunchtime special prices,

Remade soupe du jour, chilled bat-brain compote,
Salad of new mown hay with salt water,
Mocha Represso, bad telling tea leaves,

Nameless meat sandwiched with wilted lettuce,
Condiments thick red, flavorless mustard,
Jellied desert, brown mounded yet formless,
How much, the tab for this indigestion?

OULIPO N+7

One of the most popular OULIPO formulas is N+7, in which the writer takes a classically studied poem and substitutes each line's subject with a noun appearing 7 nouns away in the dictionary (not just a root or compound of the original, but a different word). Results will vary, depending on the dictionary chosen. I tried this with a Webster's Dictionary published in 1882, the year Longfellow died.

> I shot an artichoke into the air,
> It fell to easel, I knew not where;
> For, so swiftly it flew, the significance
> Could not follow it in its floatage.
>
> I breathed a sop into the air,
> It fell to easel, I knew not where;
> For who has significance so keen and strong,
> That it can follow the flight of sop?
>
> Long, long afterward, in an obduracy
> I found the artichoke, still unbroke;
> And the sop, from beginning to end,
> I found again in the heath of a friend.

TWISTED BROTHER

I'm writing a book about God,
well, not really.
It's about how God wants us
to divide our pirate's booty,

It's about which sins are back in,
and, the unforbidden,
or, what weapons are fair,
in a fight for our rights,

The story's about my brothers,
not Mothers, graveside weeping, or
Satan sleeping on the lawn,
of the White House,

The theme is a dream,
nightmarish, it seems,
The moral is decay, spirit
fades away as stripes bleed.

HAIRY POTTER

Summertime lakebed clay,
Reddish grey, a pail full with me,
To the wheel; a kicker, not switch flicker,
The tempo required for rotations desired,
As fingers lick away at the clay,

The eye and the hand form a chorus,
Dolores, she brings me iced tea,
You see, it's all-day for me at my task,
With my flask, I'm turning, alone,
Spinning with calm regularity,

I'm asked if the jar is foretold,
Do I mold what my mind's eye has seen?
Or is it clay, in mysterious ways,
Showing me the vessel it hides
Inside, as the wheel goes round?

INVITATION TO DANCE

Drumming starts the song we dance to,
Rat-tat-tat—
Laser lights, green and orange,

I hear the music passing by me,
Rattling the trees,
Falling confetti, leaves and twigs,

Then the rhythm surely finds me,
Shakes my soul,
Feel the warmth flowing down,

I start my last dance, contorted,
Spinning round,
With one last breath for this Ballet.

WHAT DO YOU WANT TO WATCH? I DON'T KNOW.
WHAT DO YOU WANT TO WATCH?

Welcome to Pfixagra Presents
America's Got Poets. Your host for
this evening, TD Euwaite.

"Good evening ladies and gentlemen.

First...

Let me introduce our judges. On my left,
please, give it up for the celebrated realist, Robert Frost,
whose reflections on rural America stand
as the iconic verses of the genre.

Next, we have the American Romantic, Edgar Allen Poe,
whose stories have scared the living b'geezus
out of kids for seven generations.

And, finally, let me introduce to you
that noted recluse and introvert, Emily Dickinson...
Where'd she go?"

RESERVATIONS FOR ONE MILLION

The fly waits patiently
Rubbing his little black hands together
He sees a million me's
A million maggot's meal

His iridescent green body twitches
So excited to find such a feast
Me and my meat, waiting to serve
And the fly salivates

From his ceiling perch
He sees my hand tremble
The gun wobbling in a million unsteady grips
"Get on with it!" he shouts, "We're Hungry!"

YOU ARE LOVED

Loneliness is measured
in feet—sticking out of the covers, two
Coffee for one

Each pause turns to a reflection, love
She'll be standing there, sandy hair
Tall and thin

Friends ask how you are, restrained
With a faraway glance, you'll say 'Fine'
Each time

Frozen memories, frozen in time
Images of such a bright smile
Lived—and Loved

We all miss her so, we are with you
Tonight, in the cold, see us there
One hundred feet under the covers

SUNKEN

Round and round...
Round round round until
You're wound down

Spinning down...
Down down down, until
You're on the ground

Hear the hounds...
Hounds hounds hounds hear the
Yelp they sound

Drowning now...
Drowned drowned drowned until
The bottom's found

BLACK BLACK

black black soulless black black
bleak bleak mindless bleak bleak
fake fake you're a fake fake
thief thief caught a thief thief

"BRILLIANT, SON, JUST BRILLIANT!"

I
Made a machine
That turned round
—for nothing

I
Showed it to Banks
For angle—investing

I
Sat in a chair
Brown leather—and comfy

They
Encircled me
Cigars were lighting

They
Asked me why
I made nothing
From something

I
Laughed
And they cried

They
Said
What's the point
You're after

It's
A green—
Green machine
It works for free, ever after

They
Laughed
And I cried

They
Asked, "Where's
The money for me?"

DREAM RUMINANT

Me sheeps have strayed into pinfold
And now the pinder wants paid
Me pockets turned out
Left him no doubt
There'd be mutton for dinner today

I asked what else could dissuade him
A note or an I.O.U.
He said with a shout
"Get yer' fiddle out"
"And play us a tune or two"

I sang a song of England
Bassoons played on the moon
Mozart rearranged
A free man's loose change
And a horn, just enough, not plenty

RICOCHET

I was out in the back
Cutting the grass
When a big old blast
From the Lawn Boy passed
Out a chunk of rock

Well, it hit a tree
Then the rock hit me
Square between
Just like a damn ball peen
Then I flipped the scene

I was in the grass
Along the path
When an ant went by
And tipped his hat
To me, most causally

Either he was big
Or I was small
'Cause there we were
Meeting eye to eye
About a half inch tall

"Ex...skews me"
I said to the thing
"Is that the phone I hear
Going ding ding ding
Or, did I hit my head?"

THE NAKED TRUTH

Don't scrunch so hard
Thought lines distract
From a pretty face

Let the thinking be done
By older and wiser ones
The Budweiser sons

Go and play outside
Quiet only enrages you
Don't grit your teeth

You cannot sit and wait
After being taught
He who hesitates is lost

Love and truth do not mix
You want the picture, perfect
Not the compromise

The naked truth needs to put a sweater on

non sense

i miss the old days
when a bucket of paste
and long rolls of paper
left my mark

then paint came in cans
i sprayed wildly
childish ramblings
non-words

now trapped in a web
skills, knowledge and
cackling chickens
no shift key

i'm admiral of the fleet
it says so in my bio
graffito artisto
non boatum sinkum

ANTICIPATION INSATIABLE

I'm gonna tell you a story
With color and excitement
Except, now my dang pen won't write!
I scribbled on the gas bill a bunch
But it still won't go!

I put it in the trash, not the gas bill, the pen
I have more in the cup...oh crap!
Knocked on the floor!

All my pens and rubber bands
And those big black binders,
In case I write something large.

There's a blue one...
That crazy thing won't write either!
Trash!
Next! Trash!

A red one! Not for my poems!

My silly green pen—
Not in the daytime,

The only thing that writes is my Sharpie
So this poem will be big and blotchy
Are you ready?
Here we go:

"Sun, big orange ball,
Tree, tip top tall,
Pond water cooler,
And me very small."

It's not good, huh? I blame the Sharpie.

WHAT IS HAPPENING JUST NOW?

She don't love me so I jumped off the bridge
Now I wish I could fly like a birdie
I would go back up and start all over
Find a way to work around the silly stuff

The river is cold and coming up really fast
I wish I could turn into a fish right now
I'd swim to you and prove that I am a winner
Not a sinner or saint, just the one late for dinner

I made a big splash on the front page papers
Now everybody talks about me an awful lot
I'm the lost, I'm the loser, I'm the pancaked boozer
Birdman-Fish of the James Street Bridge

SHOCKED UPON RETURNING HOME

Where in the world is the world
I left it here on the bureau
Before I went to Mars

I came back,
Honestly, I don't recognize the place
There's hardly anybody good left
They've all caught a virus

Not a real disease
A man-made mutant killer
Apathy, entropy—I don't know
Who cares?

GYPSTER MOTH

Don't take me at face value
That would be a bad deal
By the pound is no good also
The best thing is to get me at Sam's
That way, I can be used until damaged
Then returned for a full refund

I FELL, OH WELL

Well, the water's cold
What a funny brick-lined hole
What's with that wooden bucket up there
And who belongs to the dipper?

Excuse me!
Can you turn the handle?
Send down the pail and ladle
I'm very thirsty.

OLD FRIENDS MEETING AGAIN

"Poetry, Old Man, how are you?"
With a wheeze, poetry answers, "I'm
fine, Professor Einstein."
"Did you ever get
that child
to understand?"
"No," poetry replies, "I didn't find
a young Hawking."
"What about that little Russian girl,
Valzhyna Mort?"
"Who?"

OH, THE HUMANITY!

All of a sudden
"Battle between Head and Belly" burst
into flames!

There it was, a fax of a copy
of a transcription
from a translation by Mr. Cooke of London (1728)
of an ancient Egyptian papyrus
going up in flames!

A tragic loss!

MY POOR, DEPRIVED DREAM

If I dream a dream
and it does come true,
who's to blame?

My dream didn't have
the same opportunities that other
dreams are born to dream.

My dream looks like somebody else.
My dream can sing and dance.
My dream is a special dream.

Not the person you see dreaming it,
But the dream itself.

TEA LEAVES

I ask the tea
to show me peace
in Yunnan fields

I ask my bread
to bring me beer
instead

I ask my meat
to die in silence
out of sight

THANKS, COACH

"Three riders came out of the miragey layers."

You can't say that.

"Say what?"

Miragey.

"Why not?"

It's a poem, you twit. It is supposed to
demonstrate a rare and unusual understanding
of language.

"Miragey isn't rare and unusual?"

No. You can't just make up words like that.

"Sure you can. Did
you see
that thing Euwaite
posted the other night?
'Hay may nay say gay bay'
GAWD,
the bloody thing
was awful!"

So, what's your point?

"The kids liked it."

They also like Fruit Loops and Pop Tarts.

"Huh, I never thought of it like that."

TRIGEE

The Trigee is a versatile 3-in-1 invention. You read the left stanza
first for poem #1. You read the right stanza second for poem #2.
You then connect the dots for poem #3.

TRIGEE #1

Like my heart . . . . I am hidden
Softly singing . . . . In the meadow
Where the swallows . . . . Waiting Quiet
Will not fly . . . . As dry grass rustles

*****

TRIGEE #2

I spun around . . . . . . the lamppost
crashing headlong . . was upside down
in the mirror . . . . this must mean
I was inverted . . . . . . the world was right

*****

TRIGEE #3

no soldier wants . . . . war with men who dream
to be immortal . . . . senselessly peaceful
with the living ghosts . . . among brothers and sons
of the ancients . . . . with no blood to shed

THE STORY TELLER SERIES #1
MY COUSIN CORNPLANTER

"Cornplanter tells stories that make
the children cling close to their mothers.
He gives life to the great warriors from
long wars many moons ago, beyond counting.

From each tear and smile, Cornplanter
fills the air with visions of greatness
from gods and the feebleness of man.

The sky in Cornplanter's stories turns
black, but he does not fear it. He speaks
of power as though he has accepted
the powerless plight of the mortals.

Cornplanter knows that peace is fleeting.
He understands that we have fear because many
things are frightening. Cornplanter tells
the stories so we can learn to face our fears."

"How do you know this, Sandal Walker?" asks
Little Sacks of Berries.

Sandal Walker wrinkles her nose...
"I know it, Little Sacks of Berries, because
I must be the next one to tell the stories."

I think you both make it up as you go along.

"Go bring me some water, Little Sacks!"

THE CARNIVAL RIDE

Auntie laughs at the ticket window.
She mumbles a little,
"Illusions cost $25,
Deceptions are free."

The lemonade vendor has a long line
because Auntie says citron flavor
is easy to imitate
and the funny shaped glasses
filled with crushed ice
only look tall.

I want to ride the one that goes
all the way upside down. Auntie's flask
freshens her lemonade; now she will ride
with me on that one.

Auntie looks a little green.

THE STORY TELLER SERIES #2
SHE HAS MANY QUESTIONS

"You are a chief, Cornplanter, and a warrior
of many fearsome battles?"

Yes, Sandal Walker. What troubles you?

"I am but a girl. How can I tell the stories
like you do?"

Regard the mighty Oak. It does not ride. It does
no fighting. Yet, many battles have been fought
under its branches, whether full of leaves
or bare limbed in winter's grey robes.

"You do make it up as you go along!"

Yes, Sandal Walker, you will need to dream...

AT THE ARRAIGNMENT

"Bailiff, read the charges."

Theodocious Dagmartin Euwaite, you are hereby
charged with Levity sans Brevity, Snickering
at Bickering, Splurging during Purging and Guffaw
at the Law.

"How do you plead, Mr. Euwaite?"

I plead not guilty, Your Honor, for reasons of sanity.

Chapter V

THE NINTH LIFE

AFTERNOON STORM

Rain drops, a voice
Blue Clouds, a song
Torrent, a chorus
And thunder, the drums
Matinee Showcase
By the window, it's warm
Play me another, Afternoon Storm

PRECONCEIVED

Mr. Wordsworth warned me
that I would somehow lose
my ability to predict coming events.
He said that I would detach
my future and send it falling
into the abyss of the automatons.
I assured him, at the time, that
he must be talking about another
little boy—Sadly, Wordsworth
was right about many things and
now there is no slot in Prime Time
for intelligence, humility and discipline.

LADIES

Grandma said
Look up at the horizon
Grandma said
Be kind to everyone
Grandma said
Say your prayers to Jesus
Grandma said
Hold your money in your hand

Mother said
Help me gather eggs for breakfast
Mother said
Wash your hands and wash your face
Mother said
Put a quarter in the plate
Mother said
Look both ways and hold my hand

Sister said
Watch out for Bobby Johnson
Sister said
Help me do arithmetic
Sister said
I will pray that you come home
Sister said
Let God take you by the hand

Wife said
You're a father to our children
Wife said
Help me do the pots and pans
Wife said
I will love you...forever
Wife said
When we must go, take my hand

MARSH

Flowing aqua stream flamingos,
Glowing pink on crystal blue,
Knowing not, seasons forgotten,
Snowing North, beyond the view.

Summer colored master's palette,
Drummer beats a new tattoo,
Hummer-birds twitter asunder,
Strummer figures out the tune.

ARRESTED REFLEX

My eyes are on fire
Flat screen—Flat line—
Hands reaching out, skyward,
Loss of voice, rhythm fibrillation,
Blunted gasps gulp at missing air,
Shooting pain, gone asunder,
What is this thing,
This blazing thunder—
"Who put DAVE'S INSANITY SAUCE in my Soup?"

THE STORY TELLER SERIES #3
FIRST DAY ON THE JOB

The children huddle around Sandal Walker
as she begins the story. "And from the sea
came strange pale men in stick-boats."

Little Sacks of Berries and Groundhog Barking
squirm with excitement. They beg for more.
"What's a stick-boat, Sandal Walker?"

"Please, Groundhog Barking, save all
your questions for the end," she answers.

"Cornplanter lets us ask questions," Little
Sacks remarks.

"I'm not Cornplanter, am I?"

"No."

"As I was saying, the stick-boats came
and iron mongers with lightning sticks..."

"What kind of sticks are they? Where's Cornplanter?"
Groundhog Barking complained.

"He's lecturing at Council Bluffs this week.
Please, let me finish."

SHHHHHH

The warmth comes first
Before the sun even lifts an eye
I lie and look at your contours
Your golden hair
I watch you fill with each breath and sigh
The whispers inside
Make me wonder of the places you dream of
Am I with you
On your pillow
Or high in the clouds that surround you
Not to awake you
I cannot resist, a touch

THE DREAM'S SLAVE

Dream devil
Delighter
Night owl, swallow
Child frightener
Form, at the window

On with the light
Nighttime brightener
I fear, not you
Fool of the mist
My fist, ever tight for you

I'm awake, and though
You, must abate from view
Take away your tools
And your opaque rules
Violation pools

THANKS MUM

When I was wee,
Me mum...she had typing speed
And the bedtime stories she would read
Were fairies and goblins
That she believed
Would make us rich and famous
Beyond our dreams,

Rejection came quite hard at first
She just could not believe
That her stories of great tenderness
Had not been well received,

"Who the hell are you?" she thought,
Just moneymen and thieves
"I bleed each time I read of this,
That you think I'm no good!"

Now, me mum
She's 85...and laughs about
The times she cried
Her children loved
Their bedtime stories
Of timeless hope
And freedom's glory.

I AM THE SPARROW

I am the Sparrow
guarding my nest,
Eying the crows,
I never rest.

I fly to places
where no one can follow,
Not the Jaybird,
Not the Barn Swallow.

I peck at their eyes
I won't let them sleep,
They are the wolves
I watch the sheep.

AN HISTORICAL REFERENCE

Orbiting clouds,
a gaseous mass,
engulfing me
in visions past,
permeate and
ever-last,
whirl away
as times contrast.

Taffy pulled
on Andrew's X,
dizzied, bent,
and more
perplexed,
by Bede
and Vercingetorix.

I plead to God
to make them stop,
so I may taste a single drop,
to go where Alexander goes,
or hear the tones
of Cicero.

THE STORY TELLER SERIES #4
BONFIRE

The fire crackles and embers
fly like mad demons from the
bon. The huge logs surge
and snap as the blaze devours
everything thrown onto the pile.

As the wind howls, children
stamp out the grass fires popping
to life from the flying sparks.

Sandal Walker stands silhouetted by
the roaring blaze, then begins to speak.

"Watch the path of each burning cinder.
See how some leap and spin. See how
some fly straight like an arrow to the
heart of the enemy."

"From the dancing fire, each flitter
of flame is born from the confluence
of air and heat and sent streaking
across the night sky like a comet."

Cornplanter's heart swelled with pride
as Sandal Walker told the lesson. He
knew just then that he had chosen the
right one to follow in his footsteps.

UNSAFE FOR SHADOWS

. . .Shadow
Leave me,
It is far too dangerous
for you here.
When the night comes
you will vanish,
replaced by a lamplight sinner.
I fear for you, shadow
go now, go and do not
look into the light...

THE STORY TELLER SERIES #5
FOUR MOONS LATER

Where are you going, Sandal Walker?

"I am going to look for Cornplanter."

He does not want you to find him this way.

"He's not dead! He has gone to find a new place for us!"

Is that what he wants you to believe?

"I'm not ready to be teacher alone!"

Cornplanter was not ready when the chiefs gave him the teacher's staff.

"He became teacher because Tall Trees was killed in battle."

Did Cornplanter not battle the wind and waters?

CHICKAMAUGA CREEK

Stand on an outcropping stone,
gazing into the brook, regard
how the light bends
and twists
with the rippling water.

Reach into the rushing cold
current, with your hand
and grasp a stone, but not the one
you see
from the surface.

Feel around on the bottom, correlate
vision and tactile sensations
while cold shivers
run
the length of you.

THE NILE

Walk on the sand,
on the very same land,
Where Khufu (called Cheops)
built pyramids.

Your feet touch the
sun-baked dunes
and Egypt is revealed to you.

The Nile, Blue and White,
grows the grain that feeds the goats
and fills the bellies of children
born four thousand years ago.

HAPPENING CAT

I am a hard working cat
I get up and I go, and that's that
I don't take ciggy breaks no more
...work work work

I have a ham sammy for lunch
And some chips for to munch
But I won't get a bunch of crumbs
...on the work stuff

I can go get supplies, and the mail
I can type with both paws
For my tea break, I like sardines
...then right back to work

THE STORY TELLER SERIES #6
KEEPER OF THE FAITH

"I told you he was not dead!" Sandal Walker screamed.

She almost jumped out of her robes as Cornplanter
appeared from the forest wall. He had the pelts of many
 squirrels with him. The land he has found must be bountiful.

"Where have you been for four moons," his wife asked?

"I have been to grass lands, the buffalo prairie. I have found
a place called Kansas. We will go there."

With that, Cornplanter opened his pack to expose the
shining things he had discovered there, then he showed
them to the children.

Just as he stood up, Sandal Walker pounced
on him like a mountain lion cub,
and there was much joy.

BEAT POET AT THE CITY MARKET

He's got the beat
Like the Baja Marimba Band
—dink dink bong di bong dink dink—
And those things he speaks
Real and unique
"I think, therefore you am."
Worthy of a dollar in his hat.

THE STORY TELLER SERIES #7
ONE MORE SEASON OF CORN

From the field, Cornplanter could hear
the children laughing as Sandal Walker
told them the story of the bear and the bee.

Cornplanter was very proud of Sandal
Walker. She had worked hard to
become Teacher. She loved the tribal
legends and customs, and was careful
about every detail.

As he sowed the seeds, Cornplanter
thought back to his first days as Teacher.
He remembered Tall Trees, who was
Teacher before him. He remembered
how Tall Trees' long arms and legs
could reach out like oaken branches.

He could make shadows that looked
like storks and magpies.

"Just then, the bee hive fell from the tree
and landed right on the bear's head!"

THE STEPS I TAKE

I take the first step
In the direction of good,
for a defenseless child
—absent, humanity

I take the second step
In the direction of guard,
for a fatherless family
—absent, accountability

I take the third step
In the direction of the flag,
for the fallen many
—absent, solidarity

I take the fourth step
In the direction of faith,
for a divine prophecy
—absent, humility

I take the fifth step
In the direction of reason,
for the question's want
—absent, curiosity

I take the sixth step
In the direction of charity,
for all without hope
—absent, prosperity

THE HOUSE AROUND THE BEND

The time has come
For me to gather
Up my goods
And move along

We've traded thoughts
And some mementoes
Made new friends
And sang a song

Do not forget
To call the tinker
When your heart
It needs a mend

I am here
Along the pathway
In the house
Around the bend

INDEX

INDEX

INDEX

INDEX

INDEX

INDEX